Jazz/Rock Course

A Complete Approach to Playing on both Acoustic and Electronic Keyboards

Bert Konowitz

Jazz and rock music are an important part of today's musical scene, yet they play only a small part in most piano students' formal training. With technology taking on a more important role in many music studios, the need for a Jazz/Rock Course that offers the option of combining the acoustic piano and the electronic keyboard is evident. Look at the variety of teaching problems that can be solved by this Course: improved rhythmic ability, steadier tempo, heightened listening acuity (due to 2nd parts and electronic rhythm backgrounds), more student/teacher interaction, increased sensitivity to the stylistic demands of the music, and finally, the special word when it comes to creativity—*improvisation*. For the first time, improvisation is introduced and structured in such a way that it makes it possible for *everyone* to succeed.

This book is uniquely written to be played on either a traditional acoustic piano or an electronic keyboard. At the bottom of each page, suggestions are offered for ways that acoustic and electronic instruments may be used together: **Acoustic Jamming** suggestions offer a supportive left hand accompaniment that may be added by a teacher, a parent who plays piano, or a more experienced student. **Electronic Jamming** suggestions offer specific *sounds* and *rhythm backgrounds* that may be used when playing on an electronic keyboard. Finally, the electronic *rhythm backgrounds* may also be added as an accompaniment when performing on an acoustic piano.

While Alfred's Jazz/Rock Course is designed for individual instruction, the opportunities for varied performance experiences are expanded when used in group or class lessons. Although Jazz/Rock Level 2 is correlated page-by-page with Lesson Book 2 of Alfred's Basic Piano Library and can begin as early as page 9, it may be advisable to wait until the student is about half-way through the Lesson Book. When used this way, the Jazz/Rock Course creates a high degree of student enthusiasm by introducing a "new" sound into the piano lesson. This new sound, while being "different" when compared to what the student has been playing, is the popular and familiar sound of jazz and rock. For some students, this is just what they have been waiting for.

Also available is an optional stereo cassette tape that contains all the pieces in this book. The student will be able to hear each piece exactly as it should be played, with or without an instrumental accompaniment. You can play along with the keyboard parts and/or with the instrumental accompaniments. The *right* channel gives prominence to the keyboard part the student will be playing; the *left* channel gives prominence to an instrumental accompaniment designed to be played along with the keyboard part; by *centering* the channels, you can hear both the keyboard and the instrumental accompaniment together, at equal volume. The cassette tape ($8.95, #6245) is available from your music dealer or direct from the publisher (add $2 for postage & handling when ordering direct).

Many thanks are due to Paul Woodring who was extremely helpful in the layout of the Jazz/Rock Course. In addition, he was an excellent sounding board in sorting out complex musical questions.

 A General MIDI disk is available (5727), which includes a full piano recording and background accompaniment.

Dedicated to Jessica, Rachel, Zachary and Sarah

Managing Editor: Morty Manus
Engraving and production: Paul Woodring

ISBN 0-7390-1083-2

Cover design: Ted Engelbart
Cover photography: Dale Berman

Use after LAVENDER'S BLUE,
ALFRED'S BASIC LESSON BOOK 2 (page 9).

HI! **Jazz and Rock tell how we feel.**

Feeling Happy? Great! You can play Jazz/Rock music to express that feeling.

Feeling Sad? Sorry about that … but Jazz/Rock music can also express *that* feeling.

Whatever you may be feeling, you can express those feelings through Jazz/Rock music.

Let's start Jazz/Rock by playing FEELINGS in an easygoing, relaxed manner.

FEELINGS

Easy, relaxed tempo

You can change the mood of FEELINGS by playing it in different ways. Here are some ways to try:

   Play faster (*allegro*)…play slower (*andante*)…play louder ($\boldsymbol{f}$)…play softer ($\boldsymbol{p}$)…
   play higher (*8va*) or lower than written.

Use after page 11.

Jam Session

A Jam Session is a special time when Jazz/Rock musicians play together. Electronic and/or acoustic instruments can be used, just as in PARTY TIME and PIANO MAN below.

Play PARTY TIME using an Electronic Keyboard to play along with the Electronic Jamming suggestions below. Begin the Rhythm before playing.

PARTY TIME

With energy

ELECTRONIC JAMMING: REGISTER: Brass or Funky Synth   RHYTHM: Rock or Jazz

Now play PIANO MAN as your teacher or another keyboard player plays the Acoustic Jamming duet part suggested below. You may also add the Electronic Jamming Rhythm (above) in the background.

PIANO MAN

With a good beat!

ACOUSTIC JAMMING:

IMPROV IDEA #1: Playing with Different Dynamics

IMPROVISATION ("Improv" for short) is an important part of Jazz/Rock music. Improv is a technique which invites you to use your imagination to add some of your feelings and thoughts to a piece of music, just as you did with **FEELINGS.**

There are many different ways to change a piece of music. Let's start our improv by using **DYNAMICS** (loud and soft).

CHANGING THE MOOD

Play **FORTE** (loud) the first time.
Play **PIANO** (soft) the second time.
Improvise your own DYNAMICS the last time.

ACOUSTIC JAMMING:

(Student plays 8va)

ELECTRONIC JAMMING: REGISTER: Synth Ensemble   RHYTHM: Rock or Jazz

Improv Performance #1

KALEIDOSCOPE

A Kaleidoscope contains fragments of colored glass that are arranged so that changes of position produce a variety of colorful patterns. This piece, KALEIDOSCOPE, should be played improvising different *dynamics* to create a variety of musical colors and feelings.

Suggestions: 1st time — Play *p*   2nd time — Play *mf*
           3rd time — Change dynamics throughout the piece: *p*, *mf*, *f*.

ACOUSTIC JAMMING: (Student plays 8va)

ELECTRONIC JAMMING: REGISTER: Brass   RHYTHM: Rock or Jazz

Use after page 14.

The Jazz/Rock Sound – Blue Notes

Just as crayons or paints add color to a painting, **BLUE NOTES** are specific flatted tones used in Jazz/Rock melodies to create a special quality of sound known as "blue." To discover the difference in sound that the Blue Note makes, first play LONDON BRIDGE GOES MODERN. Then play LONDON BRIDGE GOES BLUE which uses the E♭ Blue Note (∗).

ELECTRONIC JAMMING: REGISTER: Synth Ensemble   RHYTHM: Rock/Jazz/Disco/Samba/Rhumba

Use after page 16.

Blue Note Performance Piece

TWILIGHT TIME

Notice how the Blue Notes (∗) return to their neighbor tone one half-step higher. The Blue Notes and their half-step higher tones add a special feeling that first "darken," then "lighten" the sound of this piece. That's why it is called TWILIGHT TIME.

Unhurried, smoothly

ACOUSTIC JAMMING: (Student plays 8va)

ELECTRONIC JAMMING:

| REGISTER: Brass Ensemble | RHYTHM: Rock or Jazz |

Walking Bass

Use after page 18.

The **WALKING BASS** is a Jazz/Rock left hand pattern that is used to create a rhythm background.

These four tones comprise the WALKING BASS in C Major:

It can be played in a variety of ways:

Play WALKIN' ON DOWN with the left hand. Then create new sounds by adding the Electronic and Acoustic Jamming parts.

WALKIN' ON DOWN

ACOUSTIC JAMMING:

This is the melody part.

ELECTRONIC JAMMING: REGISTER: Low Brass or Slap Bass   RHYTHM: Rock or Jazz

Walking Bass Performance Piece

BASS BEAT

ACOUSTIC JAMMING: Play the bass line an octave lower.

ELECTRONIC JAMMING: REGISTER: Synth Ensemble   RHYTHM: Rock or Jazz

Use with pages 20 & 21.

G Walking Bass

Here are the four tones that comprise the WALKING BASS in G Major:

Practice these different rhythms with the G WALKING BASS.

Dynamics make a big difference in how music makes you feel.
Add the new dynamic sign pp (very soft) as you play OPEN AND CLOSE.

OPEN AND CLOSE

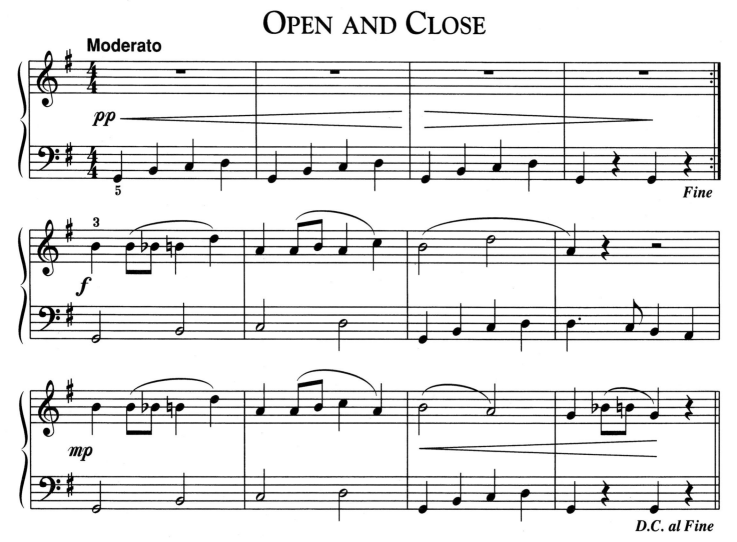

ACOUSTIC JAMMING: Play the bass line an octave lower.

ELECTRONIC JAMMING: | REGISTER: Piano or Percuss 2 | RHYTHM: Rock or Jazz

Change the dynamics on line 1 by sliding the MASTER VOLUME lever with the right hand.

G Walking Bass Performance Piece

THIS TRAIN

Memorize this piece and then let your imagination take you to all those special places that THIS TRAIN can visit.

Slowly…getting gradually faster, like a train starting out…then keep it steady.

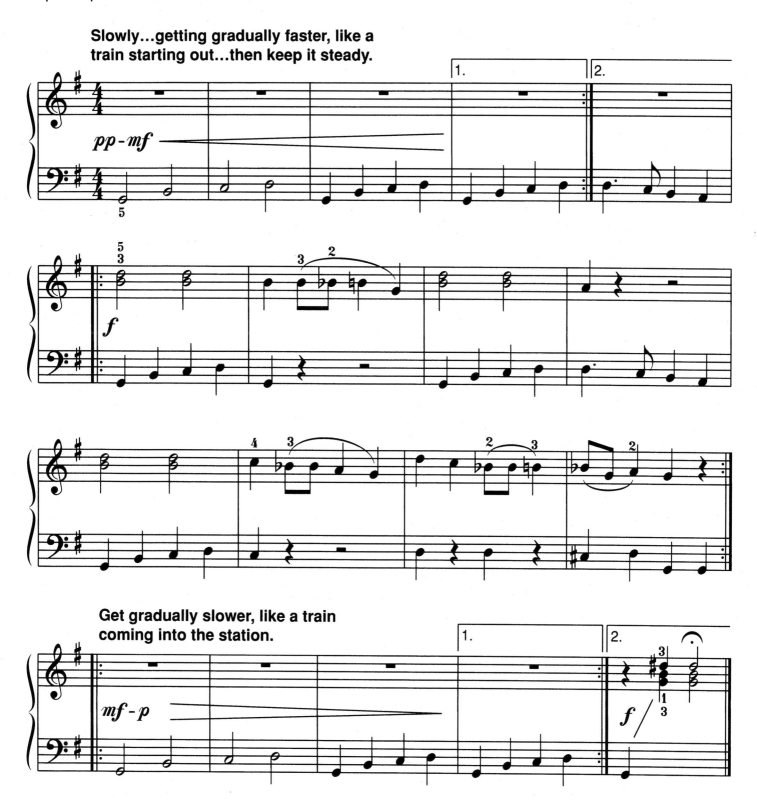

ACOUSTIC JAMMING: Play the bass line an octave lower.

ELECTRONIC JAMMING: REGISTER: Synth Ensemble   RHYTHM: None

Use after page 24.

IMPROV IDEA #2: Playing Rhythms Different Ways

In Rock music, eighth notes are played evenly:

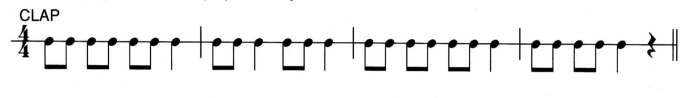

In Jazz performance, eighth notes are played a bit unevenly:

long   short long   short

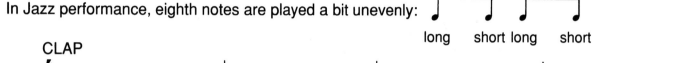

IMPROVISE

Change from Rock eighth notes to Jazz eighth notes on each repeat.

ACOUSTIC JAMMING: Use the appropriate bass as the style changes from Jazz to Rock and vice versa.

Use Electronic and Acoustic Jamming with each example on this page. Change the accompaniment to coincide with the student's eighth-note style.

ELECTRONIC JAMMING:

REGISTER: Brass   RHYTHM: Rock or Jazz, as appropriate to the improvisation

Improv Performance #2

SAM, THE PIZZA MAN

Play SAM, THE PIZZA MAN at least two times, improvising by using either Rock or Jazz eighth notes. If using the Electronic Keyboard, remember to change the RHYTHM background as different style eighth-notes are improvised.

ACOUSTIC JAMMING: Play the bass line an octave lower.
Change the accompaniment to coincide with the student's eighth-note style.

ELECTRONIC JAMMING: REGISTER: Percuss 1 or 2   RHYTHM: Rock or Jazz

Use after page 25.

The C 5-Finger Blues Scale

The C 5-finger Blues Scale has its own special sound.
Practice this example for the right and left hands.

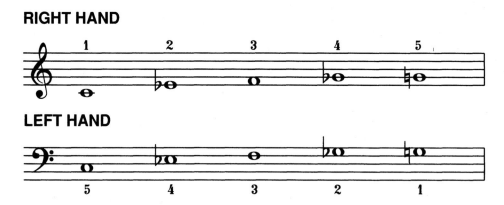

RIGHT HAND

LEFT HAND

Now discover how wonderful the Blues Scale sounds when used in a piece like BLUE STREAK.
Play in either Jazz or Rock style.

BLUE STREAK

Moderato

Play RH 8va on repeat

ACOUSTIC JAMMING: Play an octave lower. Change the accompaniment
to coincide with the student's eighth-note style.

ELECTRONIC JAMMING: | REGISTER: Synth Ensemble | RHYTHM: Rock or Jazz |

Blues Performance Piece

SUPERSTAR

Why is SUPERSTAR such a great hit? Probably because the C 5-finger Blues Scale
is used so effectively in this piece.

Repeat several times, then fade out.

ACOUSTIC JAMMING: Play an octave lower.

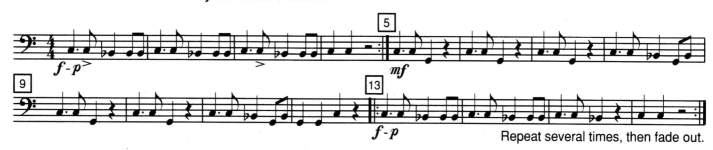

Repeat several times, then fade out.

ELECTRONIC JAMMING:

| REGISTER: Funky Synth | RHYTHM: Rock |

Use after page 27.

IMPROV IDEA #3: Creating New Melodies with the C Blues Scale

STEP 1: Review the 5-finger Blues Scale.

STEP 2: Create a *motif* (idea) from C Blues Scale tones.   Create an *ending* to the motif.

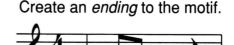

STEP 3: Use *repetition* to compose and improvise music.

EXAMPLE

IMPROVISE

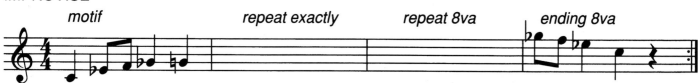

STEP 4: Create variety by playing the following 4 measures at least 3 times (in either Jazz or Rock style), as follows:

> 1st time: Improvise using exact repetition in measures 2 and 3.
> 2nd time: Improvise using 8va in measures 2, 3 and 4.
> 3rd time on: Improvise varying exact repetition and playing 8va.
> *The ending may be played either 8va or as written.*

ACOUSTIC JAMMING: Play an octave lower. Play with steps 3 and 4.
Change the accompaniment to coincide with the student's eighth-note style.

ELECTRONIC JAMMING: REGISTER: Cosmic   RHYTHM: Rock or Jazz   Play with steps 3 & 4.

Improv Performance #3

CENTERSTAGE

It's your turn to step into the spotlight, as you play the written music and improvise in the empty measures. Improvise on lines 3 and 4*, using *exact repetition* and *repetition 8va* to develop the motif. Repeat this section several times, experimenting with varied combinations and dynamics before returning to the first 8 measures. The ending measure on lines 3 and 4 may be played either 8va or as written.

ELECTRONIC JAMMING: REGISTER: Synth Ensemble   RHYTHM: Rock

Jam Session

Use after page 27.

STRETCHING OUT

A motif is usually short, so it is common to *extend* it by adding some new notes and rhythms.
The *extensions* in measures 2, 4 and 6 show how it is done. Improvise in measures 19-20 and 23-24
by using *exact repetition* and *8va repetition*. Play in either Jazz or Rock style.

Moderately slow

ACOUSTIC JAMMING: Student plays 8va. Change the accompaniment
to coincide with the student's eighth-note style.

ELECTRONIC JAMMING:
REGISTER: Brass or Percuss 2 RHYTHM: Rock, Jazz or Reggae

IMPROV SECTION

*Improvise using indicated directions.

Use after page 29.

The G Blues Scale

The 5-finger **G BLUES SCALE** is created in the same way as the 5-finger C Blues Scale.

Now practice and learn the G BLUES SCALE by first playing it several times, then changing the ORDER and RHYTHM of the tones in the scale. Then play SCAT MAN in either Jazz or Rock style.*

SCAT MAN

Not too fast

Who can sing so fast that you can hard - ly tell what's sung? Scat man can! Scat man can!

Sing - ing scat words fast - er than a fall - ing star, Scat man can! Scat man can!

Fine

Doot. Do - be do - be do - be da! Do - be do - be do

ba! Do - be do - be Scat man can! Scat man can!

D.C. al Fine

*Scat = special syllables that Jazz/Rock singers use when there are
no words to a melody, or when improvising new melodies.

ACOUSTIC JAMMING: Play the left hand an octave lower. Change the accompaniment
to coincide with the student's eighth-note style.

ELECTRONIC JAMMING: | REGISTER: Jazz Organ | RHYTHM: Rock, Jazz or Bossa Nova

G Blues Performance Piece

SPEAK UP

The G Blues Scale and the G Major Scale combine to create an exciting melody. Use your improv skills by playing some of the repeated motifs 8va on the repeat. Then experiment by playing 8va in new places. As an example, play lines 3 and 4 8va on the repeat. You will add a great sound by improvising the dynamics of SPEAK UP along with the 8va improv.

ACOUSTIC JAMMING: Student plays in Jazz or Rock style. Change the accompaniment to coincide with the student's eighth-note style.

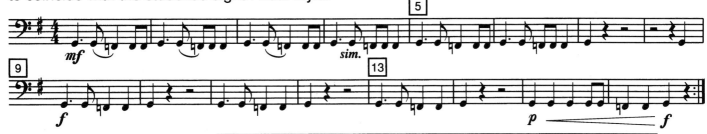

ELECTRONIC JAMMING: | REGISTER: Funky Synth | RHYTHM: Rock, Jazz or Salsa

IMPROV IDEA #4: Creating New Melodies with the G Blues Scale

STEP 1: Play as written:

Now play it backwards:

Retrograde means to play backwards.

STEP 2: Expanding a motif using *retrograde*.

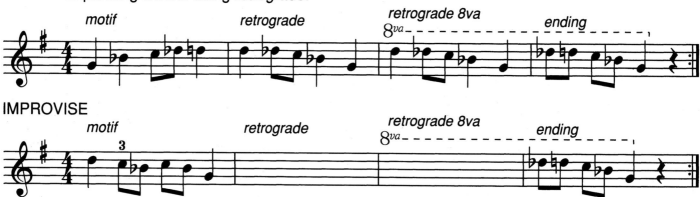

IMPROVISE

STEP 3: Using *retrograde* of a written motif to create an improv.

Play line 1 as written, completing line 2 by improvising *retrograde* and *8va retrograde* of the motif in the empty measures.

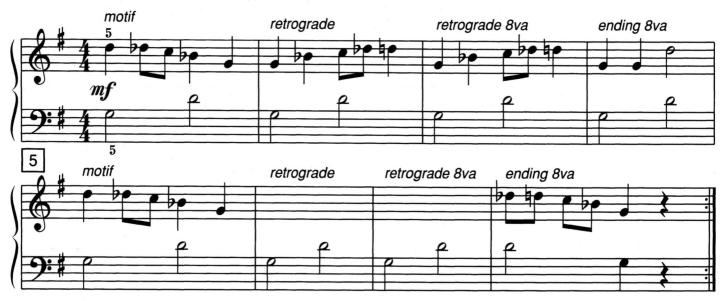

ACOUSTIC JAMMING: Student plays in Jazz or Rock style. Change the accompaniment to coincide with the student's eighth-note style. Play with steps 2 & 3.

ELECTRONIC JAMMING: REGISTER: Cosmic   RHYTHM: Rock or Jazz

Improv Performance #4

BACK WOODS BOOGIE

The Boogie bass is a popular Jazz left hand pattern. It is used here as a background to play against a motif and its retrograde. First learn this bass line:

LH WARM-UP:

After you have learned this piece, practice the improvisation on the last line as follows:
    1st time: *repetition* and *repetition 8va*.   2nd time: *retrograde* and *retrograde 8va*.

IMPROVISATION SECTION

Repeat, then D.C. al fade out

ACOUSTIC JAMMING: Play the left hand an octave lower. Use the following left hand pattern for the IMPROV section only.

ELECTRONIC JAMMING: REGISTER: Brass   RHYTHM: Jazz

Use after page 34.

Chords and the Blues Progression

THREE IMPORTANT CHORDS
USED IN JAZZ/ROCK:

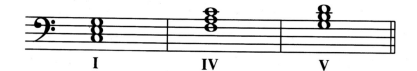

CREATING A BLUES PROGRESSION

The *blues progression* is a series of chords which usually uses the **I, IV, V⁷** chords and is generally 12 measures long.

THE C MAJOR BLUES PROGRESSION

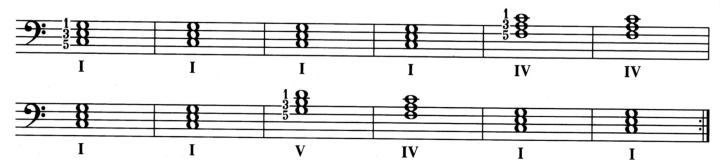

CHASING THE BLUES AWAY

Now we add a melody to the C Blues Progression and we call it the *blues.*

ELECTRONIC JAMMING: REGISTER: Jazz Organ   RHYTHM: Jazz or Big Band

BLUES FOR WYNTON MARSALIS

Use after page 34.

Wynton Marsalis is a great jazz trumpet player. He grew up in New Orleans, a city known for great blues. Wynton plays the blues with jazz groups, as well as classical music with the world's finest symphony orchestras.

Playing the right-hand eighth notes in a Jazz style will sound perfect with the Walking Blue Note bass.

Introduction

ACOUSTIC JAMMING:

ELECTRONIC JAMMING: | REGISTER: Jazz Organ   RHYTHM: Jazz or Big Band

Use after page 36.

Jazz/Rock Accents

Jazz/Rock music is often played with an accent (>) on the 2nd and 4th beat in the measure. An accent means you play the note louder. Here's what it looks and feels like.

JAZZ/ROCK ACCENT WARM-UP

Say and Clap:

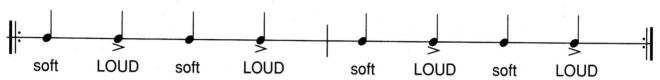

soft LOUD soft LOUD soft LOUD soft LOUD

KEYBOARD WARM-UP

RED HOT ACCENTS

To make the 2nd and 4th beat in the measure really sizzle, make the LH 1st and 3rd beats soft and short.

ACOUSTIC JAMMING: Student plays in Jazz or Rock style. Play the left hand an octave lower. Change the accompaniment to coincide with the student's eighth-note style.

ELECTRONIC JAMMING: REGISTER: Synth or Percuss 2   RHYTHM: Rock or Jazz

EASY DOES IT

Jazz/Rock accents are used on lines 1 and 2. To create a pretty contrast, play lines 3 and 4 without accents. Why not experiment and add or take out accents at various other places?

Play the eighth notes in a Jazz style — it will really sound lazy that way!

ACOUSTIC JAMMING:

ELECTRONIC JAMMING: REGISTER: Flute/Clarinet/Electric Piano   RHYTHM: Jazz

Left Hand Melody

Use after page 38.

This *ballad* (a slow composition with a singable melody) requires that the melody be played louder (*mf*) in whichever hand it is found (LH in lines 1, 2; RH in lines 3, 4).

HEARTBROKEN

ELECTRONIC JAMMING: | REGISTER: Piano RHYTHM: Slow Rock

Left Hand Rhythm

JET PLANE BOOGIE

This jet plane uses a Blues Progression to take you almost anywhere you would like to go.
Press the Rhythm button on an electronic keyboard and you are off to the location indicated below.
If you change from one rhythm to another, you have created a great trip for yourself!

ELECTRONIC JAMMING: REGISTER: Funky Synth

RHYTHM:	PLACE:
Rock	London, England
Jazz	New York City
Bossa Nova, Salsa	South America
Country	Nashville, Tennessee
Disco	Los Angeles, California
March	Main Street, USA
Heavy Metal/16 Beat	Your Home Town

WARM-UP: Boogie Bass

ACOUSTIC JAMMING: Play left hand an octave lower.

30

Use after page 41.

IMPROV IDEA #5: Creating an Added Section for Improvising

Jazz/Rock musicians often add a new section at the end of a piece of music so they can improvise new melodies and rhythms. This is done to make a performance more interesting.

DOWNTOWN

STEP 1: Play the music as written.

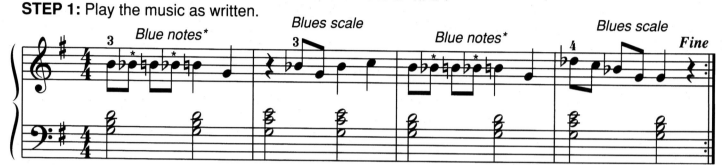

Repeat each time

Remember that the B♭ *blue note* (∗) must return to its B♮ neighbor tone ½ step higher. When the B♭ is used in the Blues Scale, it can go to *any* tone in the Blues Scale.

STEP 2: Repeat measures 1-4 of DOWNTOWN, playing only the left hand.

Play one time and go on to Step 3.

STEP 3: Examine the melody of DOWNTOWN (step 1). Measures 1 & 3 use the B♭ *blue note*. Measures 2 & 4 use tones from the 5-finger Blues Scale (review page 20). Improvise in measures 3 & 4 (below) using *repeat, retrograde, 8va* or any tones of the *blues scale*. The only rule is to end the piece on G. Play steps 1, 2 and 3 as a complete, continuous performance.

*Repeat, then
D.C. al Fine*

Use Acoustic and Electronic Jamming with each example on this page.

ACOUSTIC JAMMING:

ELECTRONIC JAMMING: | REGISTER: Brass/Cosmic/Percuss 2 | RHYTHM: Rock/Jazz/Salsa

Improv Performance #5

COOKIE JAR

What to play in Add-on Improv: *Blue Notes/Blues Scales, Repetition, Retrograde, 8va.*
How to play throughout the piece: Vary the Dynamics and select either Rock or Jazz eighth notes.

Fine

repeat several times, then D.C. al Fine

ACOUSTIC JAMMING: Play an octave lower.

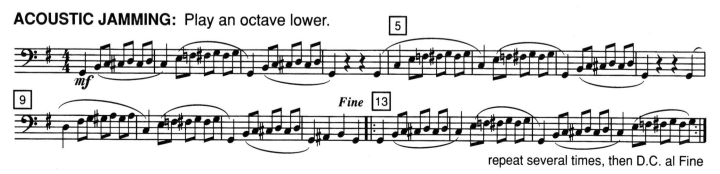

repeat several times, then D.C. al Fine

ELECTRONIC JAMMING: REGISTER: Jazz Guitar   RHYTHM: Rock/Jazz/Salsa

Summary of Improv Ideas and Performance Pieces

IMPROV IDEA	PAGE	PERFORMANCE PIECE	PAGE
1. Playing with Different Dynamics •Playing *p*, *mf*, *f*	4	KALEIDOSCOPE	5
2. Playing Rhythms Different Ways •Playing Rock Style Eighth Notes *e - ven e - ven etc.* •Playing Jazz Style Eighth Notes *long short long short etc.*	12	SAM, THE PIZZA MAN	13
3. Creating New Melodies with the C Blues Scale •Creating a Motif •Improvising by using repetition of the motif •Improvising by using 8va repetition of the motif	16	CENTERSTAGE	17
4. Creating New Melodies with the G Blues Scale •Creating a Motif •Improvising by using retrograde of the motif •Improvising by using retrograde 8va of the motif	22	BACK WOODS BOOGIE	23
5. Creating an Added Section for Improvising •Improvising with Blue Notes* •Improvising with the Blues Scale	30	COOKIE JAR	31